ALOHA!

**As we say in hawaii
"E Komo Mai"
Come in and enjoy**

Animal Riddles
from
The Ocean

Are you a curious child?
If so...
I wrote and photo-illustrated
this book just for YOU.

Tamara Montgomery

dedicated to
"The Originals"
Pat Fujioka Reiko Ho,Lisa Matsumoto,Natalie McKinney
Thank you for years of personal and creative support.

Tutu's Tips

Tutu is the Hawaian word for Grandmother

This book is designed to introduce children
to animals that live in the ocean.
Here are some ideas for using this book.

1. Word Clues: Each riddle contains word
clues that hint at each animal's appearance
or behavior; "disguised like a tree, bubble
of trouble, sees half of me." Explore these
words and how they relate to the animals.

2. Movement: Children love to move and
act things out. Encourage them to become
a sea animal; move like an octopus through
the water, scurry across the sand like a
crab, or blow up like a pufferfish.

3. Create Riddles: Make up a riddle about
sea animals that are not in this book.

The Animals Inside

 The Sea Otter

 The Leafy Sea Dragon

 The Shark

 The Octopus

 The Jellyfish

 The Pufferfish

...and some more

The Sea Snake

The Seal

The Sea Urchin

The Crab

The Hammerhead
Shark

The Whale

Who likes to float
on top of the sea,
cracking the oysters
and eating with glee?

The Otter

Who gets a prize for
"disguised like a tree?
Just look in the
kelp leaves and soon
you will see.

The Leafy
Sea Dragon

Who has the scariest
teeth in the sea?
They're big and they're
sharp...
Please don't eat me.

The
Shark

Who has eight arms
to swim fancy free?
Spread them out wide,
so lovely to see.

The Octopus

Who is a bubble
of trouble afloat
in the sea?
Pretty to look at
but...
please don't sting me.

The
Jellyfish

Who can blow up like
a ball in the sea?
Ballooning so big...
but you can't fool me.

The
Pufferfish

Who wears black
rings and swims
silently?
I must be careful
if he comes near me.

The Sea Snake

Whose fin-footed
feet and whiskers
are key,
to finding his food
as he swims
in the sea?

The Seal

Who has sharp spines
where his body
should be?
Pointy and prickly...
Please dont' stick me.

The Sea Urchin

Whose eyes and
claws are easy to see,
scurrying 'round
on the sand
chasing me?

The Crab

Whose funny eyes are
as wide as can be?
Am I in two halves
when he looks at me?

The Hammerhead
Shark

Who waves a tail
and jumps happily,
spouting out water
and splashing with glee?

The Whale

Can you make up riddles about these ocean animals?

The Dolphin

The Ray

The Hermit Crab

The Starfish

Do you like to learn about ocean animals?

Watching, but not touching

Learning how to care for ocean animals

This ocean garden may look like flowers but they are really animals.

It is fun to discover how animals feel riding the waves.

Oceans of the World

Our planet is called the Blue Marble because most of it is covered in water. There are five big oceans filled with salt water. Because there are no roads in the oceans, animals can swim from ocean to ocean.

The Arctic Ocean

This ocean is in the north of our planet. It is very cold. Animals wth lots of fat and fur can live there. Penguins and Polar Bears like to sit on small chunks of ice when they are not swimming.

The Southern Ocean

This ocean includes Antarctica. It is very cold. Many different kinds of seals and penguins live there. Teenage penguins are brown. Big elephant seals fight for their own spot on the beach. Penguins like to ride on big chunks of ice.

Can you find the penguins?

The Pacific Ocean
This ocean is the biggest and deepest on the planet. It also has the most animals. If you were swimming in the water, you might see a sea turtle.

The Atlantic Ocean
This ocean is the second largest ocean on the planet. A long, long time ago Pirates sailed this ocean. Today explorers look for gold in the many sunken ships on the ocean floor.

The Indian Ocean
This ocean is the third largest ocean on the planet. It is also the warmest. If you swim there you will see beautiful coral reefs and fish.

Meet Dr. Tamara Montgomery

Hawaii is my home, and for forty years I was
Director of Youth Theatre and Puppetry at
the University of Hawaii. I taught puppetry
to teachers and directed plays for children.
Because I live on an island surrounded by water,
I learned to scuba dive so I could see all the
ocean animals in their natural habitat.
Once a sea turtle swam right in front of me.
I was also stung by a portuguese man o'war.
Another time two big sharks swam towards me,
so I got out of their way. The seas and oceans
are exciting places but you must be careful and
respectful of the animals when you are in their home.

Credits

Technical Design by Cliff Montgomery
Published by Tamara Montgomery Books

Acknowledgements: Sage Kupono Hunt

Images under license from shutterstock: Kris Wiktor (Sea Dragon), Tsuneo MP (Shark), Vittorio Bruno (Octopus), Judex (Pufferfish), Rich Carey (Sea Snake),Yulia Vybornyh (Crab), Michael Rosskothen (Hammerhead Shark), idreamphoto(Whale), BlueOrange Studio (Sea Turtle)
Images from Pixabay: skeeze (Sea Otter), ketchupbrause (Jellyfish), Lissi61 (Seal), Justine (Sea Urchin), claudia14 (dolphin), Mondfeuer (Starfish),SVSE (Ray), stockpic (Hermit Crab). Papafox (Polar Bear), GerDukes (Turtle),Free-Photos (Turtle), dimitrisvetsikas1969

**Turn the page
to see
my other books**

Tamara Montgomery's Books
Available on Amazon

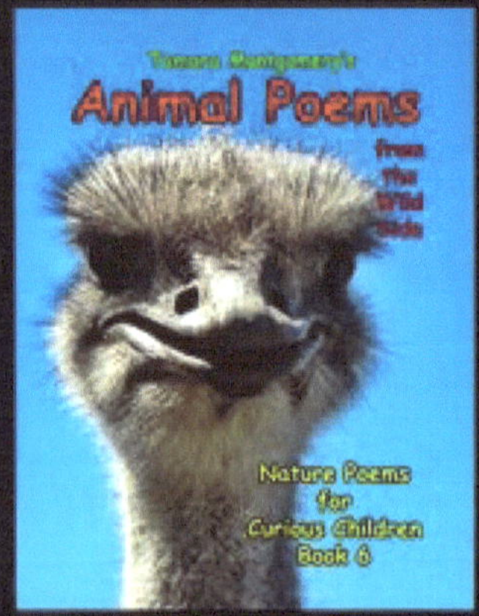

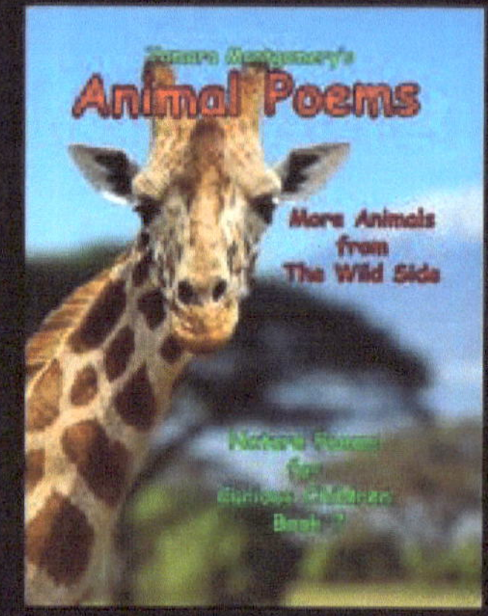

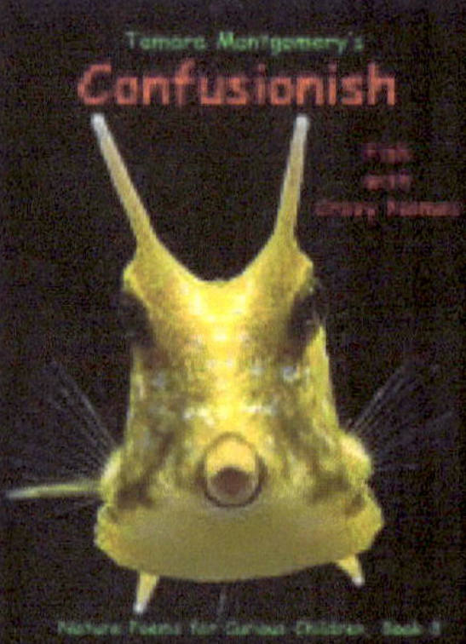

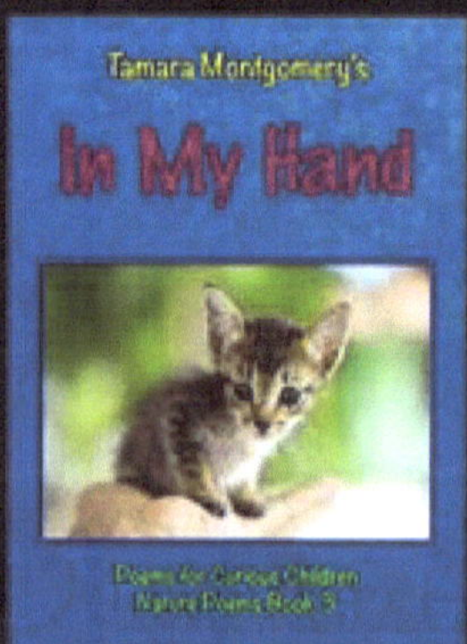

Books about Art and Color

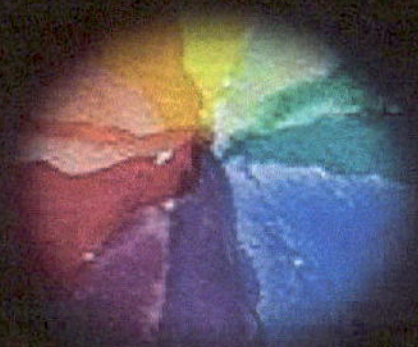

**Available
on
Amazon**

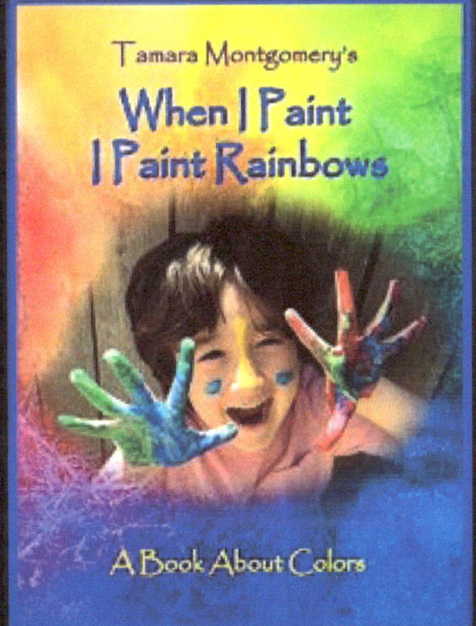

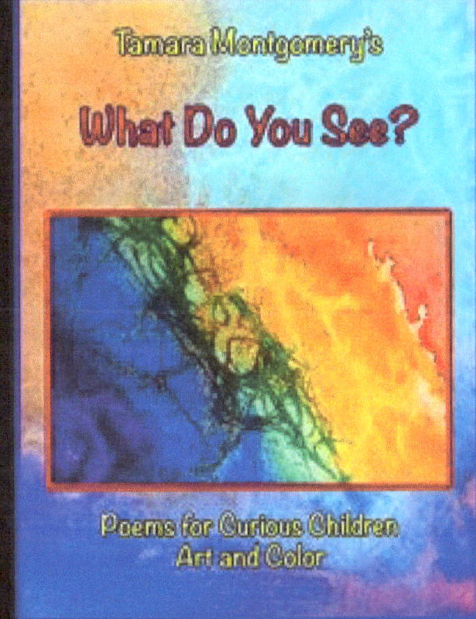

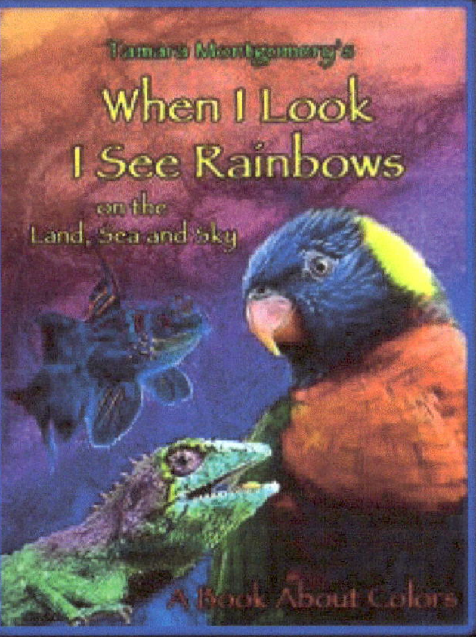